Hey Buddy, Let's Journal Together

Hey Buddy, Let's Journal Together

A light-hearted Mother & Son Journaling Experience

Tawanna S. Cullen
Adrian Matsuno

Disclaimer
The information in this book was correct at the time of publication, but the Authors do not assume any liability for loss or damage caused by errors or omissions.

©2022 by Tawanna Cullen and Adrian Matsuno.

All Rights reserved. No part of this book may be reproduced or used in any manner without the prior written permission of the copyright owner.

Paperback ISBN 978-0-9837595-3-9
Hardback ISBN: 978-0-9837595-4-6

First paperback edition February 2022

Edited by Adrian Matsuno
Illustrations by Adrian Matsuno
Layout and Typography by Tawanna Cullen
Typeset in Alegreya Sans, Avenir, Barbieri, Beloved Sans, Chandler42, Myriad Pro and Verdana

Printed by Kindle Direct Publishing in the USA

An imprint of Celebration Books Publishing
Eastvale, CA 92880

tawannashantelle.com

This book is dedicated to you two. It's dedicated to the devotion that you both have in getting to know each other and sharing such a great experience. We hope that you will create a keepsake out of this book and look back on it as time goes by. We hope that you continue on journaling together even after you finish this book. We hope that your mother/son relationship grows closer and stronger than ever. We hope that this journal will encourage you to share thoughts no matter how silly or serious they are. We hope that it will encourage you both to share ideas, opinions, dreams, and support each other.

This book is dedicated to both of you.

How to Use This Book

We are so excited you are journaling together! We hope this will be a fun and enlightening experience for both of you. Before you get started, here's some pointers on how to use this book.

This is a journal that you both will share. Mothers will write on one page and the sons will write on the other page. You decide on how often and how many pages you want to fill out at one time.

Mothers: When reading the questions, read them as if your son is asking you the questions, for instance, one of the questions asks, "What was it like when you were my age?" This would mean you would describe what life was like when you were your son's age at the present time.

Sons: When reading the questions, read them like your mother is asking you the questions. Take time to answer the questions and be descriptive and write from your heart. The longer the answers the more your mother gets to know you!

This is a get to know each other book. Once you fill in the page(s), you hand it off to your mother or son. Read each others journal entrees and respond. It's really simple and fun to do. We suggest putting the journal in a designated spot so you know where to find it.

The first step to getting started is to create your rules! This is on the following page. Leave the rules page in the book so both of you can remember what you've agreed on. We suggest both of you make the rules so it's not just one person who is making the rules up. You both own this book and we hope it is something you will keep for a very long time and look back at in later years.

Lastly, Have fun!

This Journal Belongs To Us!

Draw, Doodle or Paste pictures on this page.

Favorite photo of us

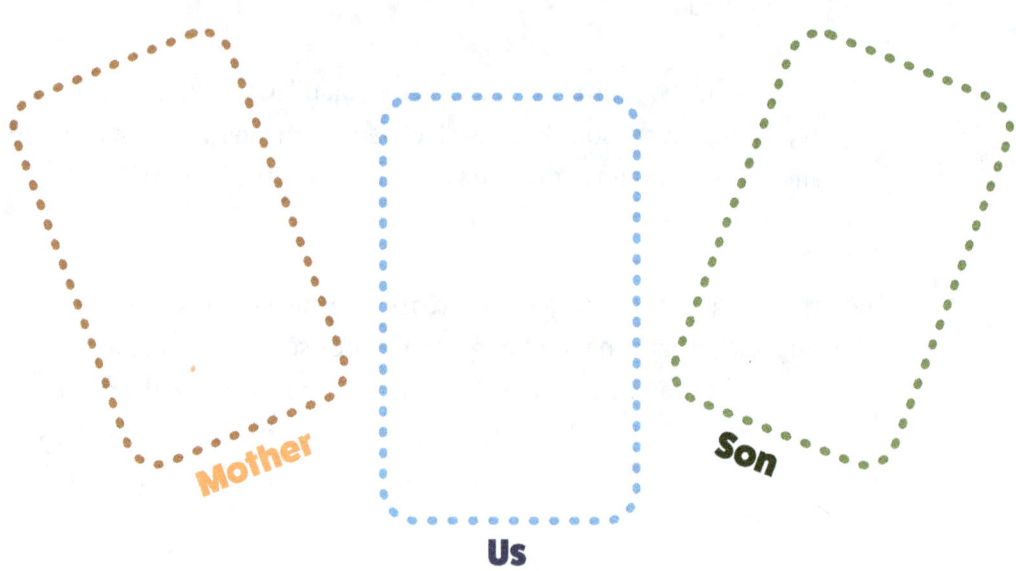

Mother **Us** **Son**

We started this journal together on:

Date: _____

A Note For Sons:

Hey I'm glad you're doing this journal with your mom! I hope you enjoy spending time to get to know your mom. Here are a few things to know about this journal and some tips on how to use it!

Your writing doesn't have to be perfect! It's alright if you don't know how to spell a word, as long as you try your best!

Take your time. Everyone goes at their own pace. You don't have to complete it in one day! You'll enjoy the experience more when you slow down and take time to think about what you are writing or doodling! Take as much time as you need!

Don't make fun of your mom's answers or doodles! If you do, then you might hurt your mom's feelings and the journal won't be as much fun.

Keep your journal conversations between you and your mom! People don't like their business all out there. I suggest limiting your serious journal conversations to be just between you and your mom because it keeps things private. You can decide that with your mom.

Be Yourself! Don't put in answers that you think your mom would like or your friends would write! You do you! This is your mom and your journal! You write and doodle whatever you like or feel!

Encourage and support each other! This is supposed to be a fun journal experience, but sometimes, things can be stressful in life so don't be afraid to write down some things you want to talk to your mom about! If your mom has something to say, listen, give her encouragement too and support her in what she writes! This is about working together, learning about each other and giving each other advice. This is not just a book to write something in, it's your own personal journal, make it special!

Spend time and cherish each moment you have with your mom! This journal is also about spending time with each other and seeing your mom's point of view on things! You get to see your moms thoughts, feelings, and creativity and she gets to see yours! Spending time with your mom can also make your relationship with her closer!
So, enjoy each moment you have with her!

I hope that you enjoy this journal with your mom! Now that we've gone through some tips, here is how you use the journal...

A Note For Mothers:

I'm so excited you're journaling with your son! I hope this will be a fun and enlightening experience for both of you. Before you get started, I would like to share a few words of encouragement and maybe a little advice.

I'm a mother of five wonderful humans and as mothers we both know our children are different and unique in their very own special way so when journaling with them, they will approach it in their own way as well. One child might write out their answers faster than you expected, while another will take their sweet time. Let them set the pace for the journaling experience to encourage a no pressure experience of journaling together. If they aren't writing to you promptly it doesn't mean they aren't interested, they may not know the answers to some questions and may need a little more time to fill out the journal. Give them ample time to answer. This may be a day, two days, or maybe even weeks at a time. I was excited to fill out my portion and hand it to them, and even more excited to get to read their answers, however, some days I had to wait.

If you are prone to correcting your son's spelling, try to refrain from grammar and spell checking in this journal. This could discourage him from writing to you. Could you imagine getting your journal back and it's been corrected like a homework assignment? That's not fun. This is a bonding journey for both of you, let the journal be a freedom space.

I would encourage conversations about the journal with your son because that allows you to get to enjoy each other more; however, I would be mindful of keeping the conversations private. This will build a bond of confidence and trust between you. What's said in the journal stays just between you and your son unless you both decide that it's permissible for both of you to talk about some of the fun things in your journal in the company of other.

Before you start journaling, you'll both need to establish rules for your journaling experience. It is important that you do this together. Let him come up with some rules so this will be meaningful to him and he can take ownership in this experience as well. There are two pages to write down rules to establish the how, when, where, why and who of your journaling experience together. Honor the rules even if he doesn't. This is a great way to model how to honor and respect boundaries and it will establish trust between you.

This journal is meant to be mostly light-hearted but don't be surprised if there are a few entries that pull at your heartstrings. Take the opportunity to offer him support if he reveals things to you, or let him know you care. It will mean a lot to him. I hope you enjoy this personal journaling experience with your son.

Shantellé

The Rules For Our Journal

This page lays out the rules for our journal. We have created these rules together and we both agree to them by signing below.

X _____ X _____
   (MOTHER)   (SON)

X _____   X _____
       (Mother)   (Son)

All About My Mother:

Today's Date: ....

Birth date: ....

Real Age: .... But I feel like Age: ....

Height: ....

Shoe Size: ....

Last Movie I watched: ....

If I could eat one food every day it would be:
....

Things I love:
....
....
....

My favorite Motto:
....
....

I want to do this journal with my son because:
....
....
....

My favorite way to spend time with my Son is:
....
....

_____
Date:

All About My Son:

Today's Date: ....

Birth date: ....

Real Age: ....   But I feel like Age: ....

Height: ....

Shoe Size: ....

Last Movie I watched: ....

If I could eat one food every day it would be:
....

Things I like: ....
....
....

My favorite Motto:
....
....

I want to do this journal with my mother because:
....
....
....

My favorite way to spend time with my mother is:
....
....

_____
Date:

Mother

My Top 3 Favorites!

My Top 3 Favorite Songs

1.
2.
3.

My Top 3 Favorite Movies

1.
2.
3.

My Top 3 Favorite Books

1.
2.
3.

Date:

SON

My Top 3 Favorites!

My Top 3 Favorite Songs

1.
2.
3.

My Top 3 Favorite Movies

1.
2.
3.

My Top 3 Favorite Books

1.
2.
3.

Date:

Mother

My Top 3 UN Favorites!

My Top 3 Disliked Board Games

1.
2.
3.

My Top 3 Disliked Songs

1.
2.
3.

My Top 3 Disliked Books

1.
2.
3.

_____
Date:

Son

My Top 3 UN Favorites!

My Top 3 Disliked Board Games

1.
2.
3.

My Top 3 Disliked Songs

1.
2.
3.

My Top 3 Disliked Books

1.
2.
3.

Date: _____

Mother

Why don't you like those board games?
....
....
....
....
....
....
....
....

Why don't you like those songs?
....
....
....
....
....
....
....
....

Why don't you like those books?
....
....
....
....
....
....
....
....

Date:

Son

Why don't you like those board games?

....
....
....
....
....
....
....
....

Why don't you like those songs?

....
....
....
....
....
....
....
....

Why don't you like those books?

....
....
....
....
....
....
....
....

Date:

What was your favorite thing to do in school or what was your favorite class?

Date:

What is your favorite thing to do in school or what's your favorite class?

Date:

Mother

What's on your mind?

Date:

Son

What's on your mind?

Date:

Mother

Doodle what your perfect house would look like outside.

Date:

Son

Doodle what your perfect house would look like outside.

Date:

Mother

My Favorite Things This Week

The best thing that happened this week:

....
....
....
....
....

My Favorite Products This Week:

....
....
....
....
....

My Favorite Everything Else This Week:

....
....
....
....
....
....
....

_____
Date:

My Favorite Things This Week

Son

The best thing that happened this week:

....
....
....
....
....

My Favorite "Stuff" Collection:

....
....
....
....
....

My Other Favorite Stuff:

....
....
....
....
....
....
....

Date: _____

Mother

Start writing a silly short story about a cat who thinks he or she is a giraffe with the best neck.

Date:

Son

Conclude the silly short story your mother wrote about the cat who thinks he or she is a giraffe with the best neck.

Date:

My Top 3 Favorites!

My Top 3 Countries I Want to Visit

1.
2.
3.

My Top 3 TV Shows

1.
2.
3.

My Top 3 Hobbies

1.
2.
3.

Date:

Son

My Top 3 Favorites!

My Top 3 Countries I Want to Visit

1.
2.
3.

My Top 3 TV Shows

1.
2.
3.

My Top 3 Hobbies

1.
2.
3.

Date:

Mother

This OR That

Circle the one you prefer.

Fish Sandwich **or** Chicken Sandwich?

Grey **or** White?

Tacos **or** Pizza?

Football **or** Basketball?

Tennis **or** Soccer?

Scooters **or** Skateboards?

Sketching **or** Painting?

Running **or** Walking?

Beach **or** Mountains?

Reading **or** Talking?

Skiing **or** Ices Skating?

Flying a kite **or** Fishing?

Water slide **or** Regular slide

Swings **or** Jungle Gym

Caramel apple **or** S'Mores?

Date: _____

Son

This OR That

Circle the one you prefer.

Fish Sandwich **or** Chicken Sandwich?
Grey **or** White?
Tacos **or** Pizza?
Football **or** Basketball?
Tennis **or** Soccer?
Scooters **or** Skateboards?
Sketching **or** Painting?
Running **or** Walking?
Beach **or** Mountains?
Reading **or** Talking?
Skiing **or** Ices Skating?
Flying a kite **or** Fishing?
Water slide **or** Regular slide
Swings **or** Jungle Gym
Caramel apple **or** S'Mores?

Date: _____

Ask Me 3 Questions:

Mother

QUESTION 1:

MOTHER'S ANSWER:

QUESTION 2:

MOTHER'S ANSWER:

QUESTION 3:

MOTHER'S ANSWER:

Date:

Ask Me 3 Questions:

Son

QUESTION 1:

....

....

SON'S ANSWER:

....

....

....

....

QUESTION 2:

....

....

SON'S ANSWER:

....

....

....

....

QUESTION 3:

....

....

SON'S ANSWER:

....

....

....

....

Date:

Mother

How old will you be in 5 years and where do you want to be in 5 years?

....
....
....
....
....
....
....
....
....
....
....
....
....
....
....
....
....
....
....
....
....
....

Date:

Son

How old will you be in 5 years and where do you want to be in 5 years?

Date:

Mother

My Favorite Things This Week

The best thing that happened this week:

....
....
....
....
....

My Favorite Products This Week:

....
....
....
....
....

My Favorite Everything Else This Week:

....
....
....
....
....
....
....

_____
Date:

Son

My Favorite Things This Week

The best thing that happened this week:

....
....
....
....
....

My Favorite "Stuff" Collection:

....
....
....
....
....

My Other Favorite Stuff:

....
....
....
....
....
....
....

Date: _____

Mother

Doodle what your action figure would look like.

Date:

Son

Doodle what your action figure would look like

Date:

Mother

My Ultimate Life Bucket List

List below the things you would love to do.

Date:

Son

My Ultimate Life Bucket List

List below the things you would love to do.

Date:

Mother

5 Quick Questions

Favorite toy growing up:

Favorite color as a kid:

Least liked color as a kid:

Favorite sport growing up:

Favorite restaurant as a kid:

_____
Date:

5 Quick Questions

Son

Favorite toy when I was 5:

....

Favorite color when I was 5:

....

Least liked color when I was 5:

....

Favorite sport when I was 5:

....

Favorite restaurant when I was 5:

....

Date:

Mother

These are my biggest fears and why:

_____
Date:

Son

These are my biggest fears and why:

Date:

Mother

My Top 3 UN Favorites!

My Top 3 Places I Never Want to Go.

1.
2.
3.

My Top 3 Disliked TV Shows

1.
2.
3.

My Top 3 Disliked Activities

1.
2.
3.

Date:

Son

My Top 3 UN Favorites!

My Top 3 Places I Never Want To Go.

1.
2.
3.

My Top 3 Disliked TV Shows

1.
2.
3.

My Top 3 Disliked Activities

1.
2.
3.

Date:

Mother

Why don't you like those places?
....
....
....
....
....
....
....
....

Why don't you like those TV Shows?
....
....
....
....
....
....
....
....

Why don't you like those activities?
....
....
....
....
....
....
....
....

Date:

Son

Why don't you like those places?

....
....
....
....
....
....
....

Why don't you like those TV Shows?

....
....
....
....
....
....
....

Why don't you like those activities?

....
....
....
....
....
....
....

Date:

Mother

What's on your mind?

Date:

Son

What's on your mind?

....
....
....
....
....
....
....
....
....
....
....
....
....
....
....
....
....
....
....
....

Date:

Mother

If you could appear in any story book, which one would you pick and what would you do?

Date:

Son

If you could appear in any story book, which one would you pick and what would you do?

Date:

My Favorite Things This Week

The best thing that happened this week:

....
....
....
....
....

My Favorite Products This Week:

....
....
....
....
....

My Favorite Everything Else This Week:

....
....
....
....
....
....
....

_____
Date:

Son

My Favorite Things This Week

The best thing that happened this week:

....

....

....

....

....

My Favorite "Stuff" Collection:

....

....

....

....

....

My Other Favorite Stuff:

....

....

....

....

....

....

....

_____
Date:

Mother

Doodle what your imaginary pet would look like.

Date:

Son

Doodle what your imaginary pet would look like.

Date:

Mother

Circle the one you prefer.

1. Did you have pets growing up?	Yes	No
2. Have you traveled outside of the country?	Yes	No
3. Can you do a cartwheel?	Yes	No
4. Do you like to run?	Yes	No
5. Do you like to wear suits?	Yes	No
6. Do you like to sushi?	Yes	No
7. Have you been to a drive-in theater?	Yes	No
8. Do you like Roller Coasters?	Yes	No
9. Do you like doing science experiments?	Yes	No
10. Can you curl your tongue?	Yes	No

Date:

Son

Circle the one you prefer.

1. Do you want pets?	Yes	No
2. Do you want to travel outside of the country?	Yes	No
3. Can you do a cartwheel?	Yes	No
4. Do you like to run?	Yes	No
5. Do you like to wear suits?	Yes	No
6. Do you like to sushi?	Yes	No
7. Have you been to a drive-in theater?	Yes	No
8. Do you like Roller Coasters?	Yes	No
9. Do you like doing science experiments?	Yes	No
10. Can you curl your tongue?	Yes	No

Date: _____

Mother

This OR That

Circle the one you prefer.

Dirt Bikes	or	4 Wheelers
Short hair	or	Long hair
Shorts	or	Pants
Suits	or	**Sweats**
Reading	or	Being Read to
Movies	or	TV Shows
Milk Shake	or	Ice cream Cone
Cats	or	Dogs
City	or	Country
Monster Truck	or	**Motorcycle**
Cartwheels	or	Jumping Jacks
Lemonade	or	Ice Tea
Yoga	or	Tai Chi
Shopping	or	Save Money
Pancakes	or	Waffles

Date: _____

This OR That

Son

Circle the one you prefer.

Dirt Bikes	or	4 Wheelers
Short hair	or	*Long hair*
Shorts	or	*Pants*
Suits	or	*Sweats*
Reading	or	*Being Read to*
Movies	or	*TV Shows*
Milk Shake	or	**Ice cream Cone**
Cats	or	Dogs
City	or	*Country*
Monster Truck	or	*Motorcycle*
Cartwheels	or	*Jumping Jacks*
Lemonade	or	Ice Tea
Yoga	or	Tai Chi
Shopping	or	*Save Money*
Pancakes	or	*Waffles*

Date: _____

Mother

What was your most embarrassing moment?

Date:

Son

What was your most embarrassing moment?

Date:

Mother

Ask Me 3 Questions:

QUESTION 1:

....

....

MOTHER'S ANSWER:

....

....

....

....

QUESTION 2:

....

....

MOTHER'S ANSWER:

....

....

....

....

QUESTION 3:

....

....

MOTHER'S ANSWER:

....

....

....

....

_____
Date:

Ask Me 3 Questions:

Son

QUESTION 1:

....
....

SON'S ANSWER:

....
....
....
....

QUESTION 2:

....
....

SON'S ANSWER:

....
....
....
....

QUESTION 3:

....
....

SON'S ANSWER:

....
....
....
....

Date:

Mother

My Top 3 Favorites!

My Top 3 Video Games
1.
2.
3.

My Top 3 Favorite Spots
1.
2.
3.

My Top 3 Favorite Sports
1.
2.
3.

Date:

My Top 3 Favorites!

Son

My Top 3 Video Games

1.
2.
3.

My Top 3 Favorite Spots

1.
2.
3.

My Top 3 Favorite Sports

1.
2.
3.

Date:

Mother

If you could relive a day or moment in your life, which would it be and why?

Date:

If you could relive a day or moment in your life, which would it be and why?

Date:

My Favorite Things This Week

The best thing that happened this week:

....
....
....
....
....

My Favorite Products This Week:

....
....
....
....
....

My Favorite Everything Else This Week:

....
....
....
....
....
....
....

_____
Date:

Son

My Favorite Things This Week

The best thing that happened this week:

....
....
....
....
....

My Favorite "Stuff" Collection:

....
....
....
....
....

My Other Favorite Stuff:

....
....
....
....
....
....

Date: _____

Mother

Create a maze for your son to solve.

Date:

Son

Create a maze for your mother to solve.

Date:

Mother

5 Quick Questions

What is your favorite dish to eat?

Where is your favorite place to read?

What is your favorite shirt?

What is your favorite quote, scripture or saying?

What is your favorite radio station?

Date:

5 Quick Questions

Son

What is your favorite dish to eat?

Where is your favorite place to read?

What is your favorite shirt?

What is your favorite quote, scripture or saying?

What is your favorite radio station?

Date:

What was the strangest dream you've ever had?

Date:

What was the strangest dream you've ever had?

Date:

Mother

This
OR
That

Circle the one you prefer.

Calling	or	**Texting**
Dinner	or	**Dessert**
Eat at Home	or	**Eat at Restaurants**
Sweet	or	**Sour**
Sunny Days	or	**Rainy Days**
Laptop	or	**Tablet**
Bears	or	**Tigers**
Travel by Plane	or	**Travel by Train**
Scary Movies	or	**Funny Movies**
Action	or	**Comedy**
Sneakers	or	**Flip Flops**
Outer Space	or	**Deep ocean**
Simple	or	**Formal**
Tokyo	or	**Paris**
Strawberries	or	**Blueberries**

Date: _____

This OR That

Son

Circle the one you prefer.

- Calling **or** Texting
- Dinner **or** Dessert
- Eat at Home **or** Eat at Restaurants
- Sweet **or** Sour
- Sunny Days **or** Rainy Days
- Laptop **or** Tablet
- Bears **or** Tigers
- Travel by Plane **or** Travel by Train
- Scary Movies **or** Funny Movies
- Action **or** Comedy
- Sneakers **or** Flip Flops
- Outer Space **or** Deep ocean
- Simple **or** Formal
- Tokyo **or** Paris
- Strawberries **or** Blueberries

Date: _____

Mother

If you could draw anything that would become real, what would you draw and what would it do?

Date:

Son

If you could draw anything that would become real, what would you draw and what would it do?

Date:

| Mother |

Would You Rather

Circle the one you prefer.

Would you rather be a character in a Marvel Movie or
Would you rather be a character in a DC Movie?

Would you rather be invisible or
Would you rather be able to fly?

Would you rather always be formally dressed or
would you rather always be causally dressed?

Would you rather be famous and rich or
Would you rather be unknown and rich?

Would you rather discover a new planet or
would you rather discover a new sea creature?

Would you rather live in a tree house or
Would you rather live in a house on the sea?

Would you rather fight in a zombie apocalypse or
would you rather fight in a robot apocalypse?

Date:

Would You Rather

Son

Circle the one you prefer.

Would you rather be a character in a Marvel Movie or
Would you rather be a character in a DC Movie?

Would you rather be invisible or
Would you rather be able to fly?

Would you rather always be formally dressed or
would you rather always be causally dressed?

Would you rather be famous and rich or
Would you rather be unknown and rich?

Would you rather discover a new planet or
would you rather discover a new sea creature?

Would you rather live in a tree house or
Would you rather live in a house on the sea?

Would you rather fight in a zombie apocalypse or
would you rather fight in a robot apocalypse?

Date: _____

Mother

What's on your mind?

Date:

Son

What's on your mind?

Date:

Mother

My Favorite Things This Week

The best thing that happened this week:

....
....
....
....
....

My Favorite Products This Week:

....
....
....
....
....

My Favorite Everything Else This Week:

....
....
....
....
....
....
....

_____
Date:

Son

My Favorite Things This Week

The best thing that happened this week:

....
....
....
....
....

My Favorite "Stuff" Collection:

....
....
....
....
....

My Other Favorite Stuff:

....
....
....
....
....
....
....

_____
Date:

Mother

Ask Me 3 Questions:

QUESTION 1:

....

....

MOTHER'S ANSWER:

....

....

....

....

QUESTION 2:

....

....

MOTHER'S ANSWER:

....

....

....

....

QUESTION 3:

....

....

MOTHER'S ANSWER:

....

....

....

....

_____
Date:

Ask Me 3 Questions: Son

QUESTION 1:

SON'S ANSWER:

QUESTION 2:

SON'S ANSWER:

QUESTION 3:

SON'S ANSWER:

Date: _____

Mother

What historical person would you want to spend the day with? Describe a perfect day with them.

Date:

Son

What historical person would you want to spend the day with? Describe a perfect day with them.

....
....
....
....
....
....
....
....
....
....
....
....
....
....
....
....
....
....
....
....
....
....

Date:

Mother

Doodle lots of your favorite shapes.

Date:

Son

Doodle lots of your favorite shapes.

Date:

Mother

My Top 3 UNFavorites!

My Top 3 Disliked Video Games

1.
2.
3.

My Top 3 Disliked Spots

1.
2.
3.

My Top 3 Disliked Sports

1.
2.
3.

Date:

Son

My Top 3 UN Favorites!

My Top 3 Disliked Video Games

1.
2.
3.

My Top 3 Disliked Spots

1.
2.
3.

My Top 3 Disliked Sports

1.
2.
3.

Date:

Mother

Why don't you like those video games?

....
....
....
....
....
....
....
....

Why don't you like those spots?

....
....
....
....
....
....
....
....

Why don't you like those sports?

....
....
....
....
....
....
....
....

_____
Date:

Son

Why don't you like those video games?

....
....
....
....
....
....
....

Why don't you like those spots?

....
....
....
....
....
....
....

Why don't you like those sports?

....
....
....
....
....
....
....

Date: _____

Mother

If you could assign each person in your family superpowers, who would get what power and why?

Date:

If you could assign each person in your family superpowers, who would get what power and why?

Date:

Mother

5 Quick Questions

1. What is/was your favorite subject in school?

2. What is your favorite chip flavor?

3. What is your favorite dance move?

4. What is your favorite magazine?

5. Who would you swap lives with for 24 hours?

Date:

5 Quick Questions

Son

What is/was your favorite subject in school?

What is your favorite chip flavor?

What is your favorite dance move?

What is your favorite magazine?

Who would you swap lives with for 24 hours?

Date:

My Favorite Things This Week

The best thing that happened this week:

....
....
....
....
....

My Favorite Products This Week:

....
....
....
....

My Favorite Everything Else This Week:

....
....
....
....
....
....
....

_____
Date:

Son

My Favorite Things This Week

The best thing that happened this week:

....

....

....

....

My Favorite "Stuff" Collection:

....

....

....

....

My Other Favorite Stuff:

....

....

....

....

....

_____
Date:

Mother

Doodle awesome bugs.

Date:

Son

Doodle awesome bugs.

Date:

Mother

Ask Me 3 Questions:

QUESTION 1:

....
....

MOTHER'S ANSWER:

....
....
....
....

QUESTION 2:

....
....

MOTHER'S ANSWER:

....
....
....
....

QUESTION 3:

....
....

MOTHER'S ANSWER:

....
....
....
....

_____
Date:

Ask Me 3 Questions: **Son**

QUESTION 1:

....
....

SON'S ANSWER:

....
....
....
....

QUESTION 2:

....
....

SON'S ANSWER:

....
....
....
....

QUESTION 3:

....
....

SON'S ANSWER:

....
....
....
....

Date:

Describe your perfect vacation.

Date:

Son

Describe your perfect vacation.

Date:

Mother

My Top 3 Favorites!

My Top 3 Candies

1.
2.
3.

My Top 3 Favorite Animals

1.
2.
3.

My Top 3 Favorite Instruments

1.
2.
3.

Date:

Son

My Top 3 Favorites!

My Top 3 Candies

1.
2.
3.

My Top 3 Favorite Animals

1.
2.
3.

My Top 3 Favorite Instruments

1.
2.
3.

Date:

Mother

Circle the one you prefer.

1. Have you ever thought about changing your name?	YES	NO
2. Have you cried while watching a movie?	YES	NO
3. Can you sew?	YES	NO
4. If you found a wallet of money would you return it?	YES	NO
5. Have you ever been fishing?	YES	NO
6. Do you like flying kites?	YES	NO
7. Do you like making S'mores?	YES	NO
8. Have you ever been ice skating?	YES	NO
9. Have you ever picked apples off of a tree?	YES	NO
10. Do you like water slides?	YES	NO

_____
Date:

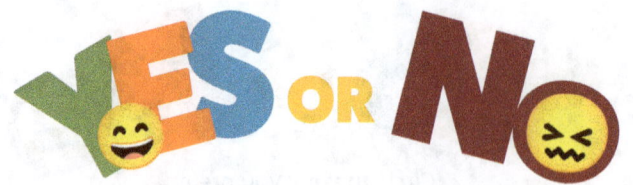

Son

Circle the one you prefer.

1. Have you ever thought about changing your name?   YES   NO

2. Have you cried while watching a movie?   YES   NO

3. Can you sew?   YES   NO

4. If you found a wallet of money would you return it?   YES   NO

5. Have you ever been fishing?   YES   NO

6. Do you like flying kites?   YES   NO

7. Do you like making S'mores?   YES   NO

8. Have you ever been ice skating?   YES   NO

9. Have you ever picked apples off of a tree?   YES   NO

10. Do you like water slides?   YES   NO

Date:

Mother

What's on your mind?

Date:

Son

What's on your mind?

Date:

Mother

If you could time travel, where would you go and what time period would you go to?

Date:

Son

If you could time travel, where would you go and what time period would you go to?

Date:

My Favorite Things This Week

The best thing that happened this week:

....
....
....
....
....

My Favorite Products This Week:

....
....
....
....
....

My Favorite Everything Else This Week:

....
....
....
....
....
....
....

_____
Date:

Son

My Favorite Things This Week

The best thing that happened this week:

....
....
....
....
....

My Favorite "Stuff" Collection:

....
....
....
....
....

My Other Favorite Stuff:

....
....
....
....
....
....
....

_____
Date:

Mother

Doodle your favorite patterns.

Date:

Son

Doodle your favorite patterns.

Date:

Mother

5 Quick Questions

Who inspires you?

Would you trade looks for intelligence or intelligence for looks?

If you had a warning label what would it say?

Would you be the worst player on the best team or the best player on the worst team?

If you joined the circus, what would you do?

Date:

5 Quick Questions

Son

Who inspires you?
....

Would you trade some looks for intelligence or intelligence for looks?
....

If you had a warning label what would it say?
....

Would you be the worst player on the best team or the best player on the worst team?
....

If you joined the circus, what would you do?
....

Date:

Mother

What do you think your strongest qualities are?
What are your son's strongest qualities?

....
....
....
....
....
....
....
....
....
....
....
....
....
....
....
....
....
....
....
....
....
....
....

Date:

Son

What do you think your strongest qualities are? What are your mother's strongest qualities?

Date:

Mother

My Top 3 Favorites!

Top 3 Favorite Colors

1.
2.
3.

Top 3 Favorite Shapes

1.
2.
3.

My Top 3 Favorite Fruits

1.
2.
3.

Date:

My Top 3 Favorites!

Son

Top 3 Favorite Colors

1.
2.
3.

Top 3 Favorite Shapes

1.
2.
3.

My Top 3 Favorite Fruits

1.
2.
3.

Date:

Mother

Would You Rather

Circle the one you prefer.

Would you rather sneeze constantly or
Would you rather drool constantly?

Would you rather have a robot clean your house daily or
Would you rather have a robot cook your food daily?

Would you rather only respond with emojis or
would you rather only respond with gifs?

Would you rather be stuck snowed in the mountains or
Would you rather be stuck in a heatwave in the desert?

Would you rather be in a world wide sing off with a hoarse voice or
would you rather be in a world wide dance off with a broken leg?

Would you rather run at 110 miles per hour or
Would you rather fly at 25 miles per hour?

Would you rather be stuck in a food fight or
would you rather be stuck in a water balloon fight?

_____
Date:

Would You Rather

Son

Circle the one you prefer.

Would you rather sneeze constantly or
Would you rather drool constantly?

Would you rather have a robot clean your house daily or
Would you rather have a robot cook your food daily?

Would you rather only respond with emojis or
would you rather only respond with gifs?

Would you rather be stuck snowed in the mountains or
Would you rather be stuck in a heatwave in the desert?

Would you rather be in a world wide sing off with a hoarse voice or
would you rather be in a world wide dance off with a broken leg?

Would you rather run at 110 miles per hour or
Would you rather fly at 25 miles per hour?

Would you rather be stuck in a food fight or
would you rather be stuck in a water balloon fight?

Date:

Mother

Doodle cars, bikes, skateboards and scooters.

Date:

Doodle cars, bikes, skateboards and scooters.

Date:

Mother

My Favorite Things This Week

The best thing that happened this week:

....
....
....
....
....

My Favorite Products This Week:

....
....
....
....
....

My Favorite Everything Else This Week:

....
....
....
....
....
....
....

_____
Date:

Son

My Favorite Things This Week

The best thing that happened this week:

....
....
....
....
....

My Favorite "Stuff" Collection:

....
....
....
....
....

My Other Favorite Stuff:

....
....
....
....
....
....
....

_____
Date:

Mother

What was life like when you were your son's age?

Date:

Son

What do you think life will be like when you are your mother's age?

Date:

My Top 3 UN Favorites!

My Top 3 Disliked Bugs
1.
2.
3.

My Top 3 Disliked Fruits or Veggies
1.
2.
3.

My Top 3 Disliked Subjects
1.
2.
3.

Date:

Son

My Top 3 UN Favorites!

My Top 3 Disliked Bugs

1.
2.
3.

My Top 3 Disliked Fruits or Veggies

1.
2.
3.

My Top 3 Disliked Subjects

1.
2.
3.

Date: _____

Mother

Why don't you like those bugs?

```
............................................................................................
............................................................................................
............................................................................................
............................................................................................
............................................................................................
............................................................................................
............................................................................................
............................................................................................
```

Why don't you like those fruits or veggies?

```
............................................................................................
............................................................................................
............................................................................................
............................................................................................
............................................................................................
............................................................................................
............................................................................................
............................................................................................
```

Why don't you like those subjects?

```
............................................................................................
............................................................................................
............................................................................................
............................................................................................
............................................................................................
............................................................................................
............................................................................................
............................................................................................
```

Date:

Why don't you like those bugs?
....
....
....
....
....
....
....

Why don't you like those fruits or veggies?
....
....
....
....
....
....
....

Why don't you like those subjects?
....
....
....
....
....
....
....

Date: _____

Ask Me 3 Questions:

QUESTION 1:
....
....

MOTHER'S ANSWER:
....
....
....
....

QUESTION 2:
....
....

MOTHER'S ANSWER:
....
....
....
....

QUESTION 3:
....
....

MOTHER'S ANSWER:
....
....
....
....

_____
Date:

Ask Me 3 Questions: Son

QUESTION 1:

....
....

SON'S ANSWER:

....
....
....
....

QUESTION 2:

....
....

SON'S ANSWER:

....
....
....
....

QUESTION 3:

....
....

SON'S ANSWER:

....
....
....
....

Date: _____

Mother

What are some things about your son that make you smile?

Date:

Son

What are some things about your mother that make you smile?

Date:

 Mother

Circle the one you prefer.

1. Do you like staying in hotels?	YES	NO
2. Have you ever been camping?	YES	NO
3. Do you like camping?	YES	NO
4. Do you like spicy food?	YES	NO
5. Have you ever met someone famous?	YES	NO
6. Are you a thrill seeker?	YES	NO
7. Do spiders scare you?	YES	NO
8. Have you ever been bullied?	YES	NO
9. Have you ever cheated on a test?	YES	NO
10. Have you ever stood up for a friend?	YES	NO

_____
Date:

YES OR NO

Son

Circle the one you prefer.

1. Do you like staying in hotels? YES NO

2. Have you ever been camping? YES NO

3. Do you like camping? YES NO

4. Do you like spicy food? YES NO

5. Have you ever met someone famous? YES NO

6. Are you a thrill seeker? YES NO

7. Do spiders scare you? YES NO

8. Have you ever been bullied? YES NO

9. Have you ever cheated on a test? YES NO

10. Have you ever stood up for a friend? YES NO

Date: _____

Mother

Doodle Outer Space things.

Date:

Son

Doodle Outer Space things.

Date:

My Favorite Things This Week

The best thing that happened this week:

....
....
....
....
....

My Favorite Products This Week:

....
....
....
....
....

My Favorite Everything Else This Week:

....
....
....
....
....
....
....

_____
Date:

Son

My Favorite Things This Week

The best thing that happened this week:

....
....
....
....
....

My Favorite "Stuff" Collection:

....
....
....
....
....

My Other Favorite Stuff:

....
....
....
....
....
....
....

Date: _____

Mother

What can your son do to become the best person he can be?

Date:

Son

What can your mother do to become the best person she can be?

Date:

`Mother`

This OR That

Circle the one you prefer.

Cartoons **or** Live Action
Art **or** Math
Plan it **or** Wing it
Backpack **or** Suitcase
Early Bird **or** Night Owl
Sunrise **or** Sunset
Dreamer **or** Realist
Always early **or** Always Late
Vanilla **or** Chocolate
Talk to All Animals **or** Speak All Languages
Be Invisible **or** Fly
Socks **or** Bare Feet
Sun **or** Moon
Ice Cream **or** Gelato
Hot Dog **or** Hamburger

_____
Date:

This OR That

Son

Circle the one you prefer.

Cartoons	or	Live Action
Art	or	Math
Plan it	or	Wing it
Backpack	or	Suitcase
Early Bird	or	Night Owl
Sunrise	or	Sunset
Dreamer	or	Realist
Always early	or	Always Late
Vanilla	or	Chocolate
Talk to All Animals	or	Speak All Languages
Be Invisible	or	Fly
Socks	or	Bare Feet
Sun	or	Moon
Ice Cream	or	Gelato
Hot Dog	or	Hamburger

Date:

Mother

What's on your mind?

Date:

Son

What's on your mind?

Date:

Mother

My Top 3 Favorites!

Top 3 Favorite Seasons

1.
2.
3.

Top 3 Favorite Restaurants

1.
2.
3.

My Top 3 Favorite foods

1.
2.
3.

Date: _____

My Top 3 Favorites!

Son

Top 3 Favorite Seasons

1.
2.
3.

Top 3 Favorite Restaurants

1.
2.
3.

My Top 3 Favorite Foods

1.
2.
3.

Date:

Mother

Dear Younger Me,

_____
Date:

Son

Dear Older Me,

Date:

Mother

Doodle weather things.

Date:

Son

Doodle weather things.

Date:

My Favorite Things This Week

The best thing that happened this week:

....
....
....
....
....

My Favorite Products This Week:

....
....
....
....
....

My Favorite Everything Else This Week:

....
....
....
....
....
....
....

_____
Date:

My Favorite Things This Week

Son

The best thing that happened this week:

....
....
....
....
....

My Favorite "Stuff" Collection:

....
....
....
....
....

My Other Favorite Stuff:

....
....
....
....
....
....

_____
Date:

Mother

Would You Rather

Write your own would you rather questions for your son.

Would you rather _____
or
Would you rather _____

Would you rather _____
or
Would you rather _____

Would you rather _____
or
Would you rather _____

Would you rather _____
or
Would you rather _____

Would you rather _____
or
Would you rather _____

Would you rather _____
or
Would you rather _____

Date:

Would You Rather

Son

Write Your Own Would You Rather questions for your mother.

Would you rather ....
 or
Would you rather ....

Would you rather ....
 or
Would you rather ....

Would you rather ....
 or
Would you rather ....

Would you rather ....
 or
Would you rather ....

Would you rather ....
 or
Would you rather ....

Would you rather ....
 or
Would you rather ....

Date: _____

Mother

If you could have your own business selling anything in the world, real or fake, what would it be?

Date:

Son

If you could have your own business selling anything in the world, real or fake, what would it be?

Date:

Mother

My Top 3 UN Favorites!

My Top 3 Disliked Candies

1.
2.
3.

My Top 3 Disliked Animals

1.
2.
3.

My Top 3 Disliked Instruments

1.
2.
3.

Date:

My Top 3 UN Favorites!

Son

My Top 3 Disliked Candies

1.
2.
3.

My Top 3 Disliked Animals

1.
2.
3.

My Top 3 Disliked Instruments

1.
2.
3.

Date:

Mother

Why don't you like those candies?

....
....
....
....
....
....
....
....

Why don't you like those animals?

....
....
....
....
....
....
....
....

Why don't you like those Instruments?

....
....
....
....
....
....
....
....

Date:

Son

Why don't you like those candies?

....
....
....
....
....
....
....

Why don't you like those animals?

....
....
....
....
....
....
....

Why don't you like those Instruments?

....
....
....
....
....
....
....

Date:

Ask Me 3 Questions:

QUESTION 1:
....
....

MOTHER'S ANSWER:
....
....
....
....

QUESTION 2:
....
....

MOTHER'S ANSWER:
....
....
....
....

QUESTION 3:
....
....

MOTHER'S ANSWER:
....
....
....
....

_____
Date:

Ask Me 3 Questions: Son

QUESTION 1:
....
....

SON'S ANSWER:
....
....
....
....

QUESTION 2:
....
....

SON'S ANSWER:
....
....
....
....

QUESTION 3:
....
....

SON'S ANSWER:
....
....
....
....

Date: _____

Mother

Doodle kind words about your son.

Date:

Son

Doodle kind words about your mother.

Date:

Mother

What would you do if you were invisible?

Date:

Son

What would you do if you were invisible?

Date:

Mother

My Favorite Things This Week

The best thing that happened this week:

....
....
....
....
....

My Favorite Products This Week:

....
....
....
....
....

My Favorite Everything Else This Week:

....
....
....
....
....
....
....

_____
Date:

My Favorite Things This Week

Son

The best thing that happened this week:

....

....

....

....

....

My Favorite "Stuff" Collection:

....

....

....

....

....

My Other Favorite Stuff:

....

....

....

....

....

....

....

_____
Date:

Mother

5 Quick Questions

What is the most unpleasant sounding word?

What is the best sounding word?

If you can have a mini version of any animal, what mini animal would you have?

What is your dream job?

What is your most treasured item?

Date:

Son

5 Quick Questions

What is the most unpleasant sounding word?

What is the best sounding word?

If you can have a mini version of any animal, what mini animal would you have?

What is your dream job?

What is your most treasured item?

Date:

Mother

What's on your mind?

Date:

What's on your mind?

Son

Date:

Mother

If your son was a cartoon character, which one would he be and why?

Date:

Son

If your mother was a cartoon character, which one would she be and why?

Date:

My Favorite Things This Week

The best thing that happened this week:

....
....
....
....
....

My Favorite Products This Week:

....
....
....
....
....

My Favorite Everything Else This Week:

....
....
....
....
....
....
....

_____
Date:

My Favorite Things This Week

Son

The best thing that happened this week:

....
....
....
....

My Favorite "Stuff" Collection:

....
....
....
....

My Other Favorite Stuff:

....
....
....
....
....

Date: _____

Mother

Doodle food things.

Date:

Son

Doodle food things.

Date:

Mother

What was your favorite grade in school and why?

Date:

Son

What has been your favorite grade in school and why?

Date:

Mother

My Top 3 Favorites!

Top 3 Favorite Cars

1.
2.
3.

Top 3 Favorite Celebrities

1.
2.
3.

My Top 3 Favorite Action Figures

1.
2.
3.

Date:

My Top 3 Favorites!

Son

Top 3 Favorite Cars

1.
2.
3.

Top 3 Favorite Celebrities

1.
2.
3.

My Top 3 Favorite Action Figures

1.
2.
3.

Date:

Mother

My Top 3 UN Favorites!

My Top 3 Disliked Cars

1.
2.
3.

My Top 3 Disliked Celebrities

1.
2.
3.

My Top 3 Disliked Action Figures

1.
2.
3.

_____
Date:

Son

My Top 3 UN Favorites!

My Top 3 Disliked Cars

1.
2.
3.

My Top 3 Disliked Celebrities

1.
2.
3.

My Top 3 Disliked Action Figures

1.
2.
3.

Date:

Mother

Why don't you like those cars?

....
....
....
....
....
....
....
....

Why don't you like those celebrities?

....
....
....
....
....
....
....
....

Why don't you like those action figures?

....
....
....
....
....
....
....
....

_____
Date:

Son

Why don't you like those cars?
....
....
....
....
....
....
....

Why don't you like those celebrities?
....
....
....
....
....
....
....

Why don't you like those action figures?
....
....
....
....
....
....
....

Date: _____

Mother

My Favorite Things This Week

The best thing that happened this week:

....
....
....
....
....

My Favorite Products This Week:

....
....
....
....
....

My Favorite Everything Else This Week:

....
....
....
....
....
....

_____
Date:

Son

My Favorite Things This Week

The best thing that happened this week:

....
....
....
....
....

My Favorite "Stuff" Collection:

....
....
....
....
....

My Other Favorite Stuff:

....
....
....
....
....
....
....

Date:

 Mother

Circle the one you prefer.

1. Would you go back in time? YES NO

2. Have you ever buried a time capsule? YES NO

3. Do you believe in aliens? YES NO

4. Do you fall asleep easily? YES NO

5. Do you like doing DIY projects? YES NO

6. Do you believe in love at first sight? YES NO

7. Do you like comic books? YES NO

8. Do you like cooking? YES NO

9. Have you ever been afraid of the dark? YES NO

10. Would you ever skydive? YES NO

Date:

Son

Circle the one you prefer.

1. Would you go back in time?	YES	NO
2. Do you want to bury a time capsule?	YES	NO
3. Do you believe in aliens?	YES	NO
4. Do you fall asleep easily?	YES	NO
5. Do you like doing DIY projects?	YES	NO
6. Do you believe in love at first sight?	YES	NO
7. Do you like comic books?	YES	NO
8. Do you like cooking?	YES	NO
9. Have you ever been afraid of the dark?	YES	NO
10. Would you ever skydive?	YES	NO

Date: _____

Mother

Write an appreciation letter to your Son.

Date:

Son

Write an appreciation letter to your Mother.

Date:

www.ingramcontent.com/pod-product-compliance
Lightning Source LLC
Chambersburg PA
CBHW081138010526
44110CB00061B/2518